COACH CONFIDENCE

EXERCISES FOR KIDS

BY ZACH HORN

ILLUSTRATED BY
PATRICIA HENDY BOWLING

Dedicated to Tricia, Tyler, Chase, Conor and our angel Michael

Lift Big, Live Big!

About the Author:

Zach Horn hails from the jungles of Harrison, Ohio where he coaches his sons in football, baseball, basketball and lacrosse. Alongside his wife, Trish, they spend their free time at the local zoo and amusement parks, hiking in the woods, biking trails and staying active in whatever fun, imaginative way they can. This book was inspired by the boys' joy of reading and exercising in the mornings with their dad. They certainly hope this book helps others stay fit and sparks joy in the minds of people everywhere.

About the Illustrator:

Patricia Hendy Bowling is married to David Bowling for almost 50 years. They live and work from their small farm home studio, "Sunshine's View", in Southwestern Ohio, that they share with dogs, cats, chickens, horses, bees and fish. She likes gardening and exploring nature with her husband, children and grandchildren. Patricia enjoys watching the grandkids play sports and being involved with many of their varied activities. Patricia is the illustrator of Dirty Dingy Daryl children's books that David wrote, and is involved with the production of their comic books, WASP vs. Killer Bees. She designs and sells dolls and toys available from their Halo Toys shop. She loves and is deeply active in her traditional Catholic faith.

HEY KIDS!

My name is COACH CONFIDENCE, the action-packed gorilla.

Everyone likes toys, books, and TV shows,
but where did all the exercise go?
You need exercise every day
to keep your body feeling great.
See how many of my exercises you can do
and track your progress as you go through.

When you're finished, you will see
that it's fun to move and be healthy.
Come back tomorrow for more
and try to improve your exercise score.

When you're finished and you need a snack,
a banana or a veggie is where it's at!
Have fun, move, smile, be great!
Can you complete all of the exercises?
Let's find out, I can't wait!

Our motto here is: "Do your best and pound your chest."

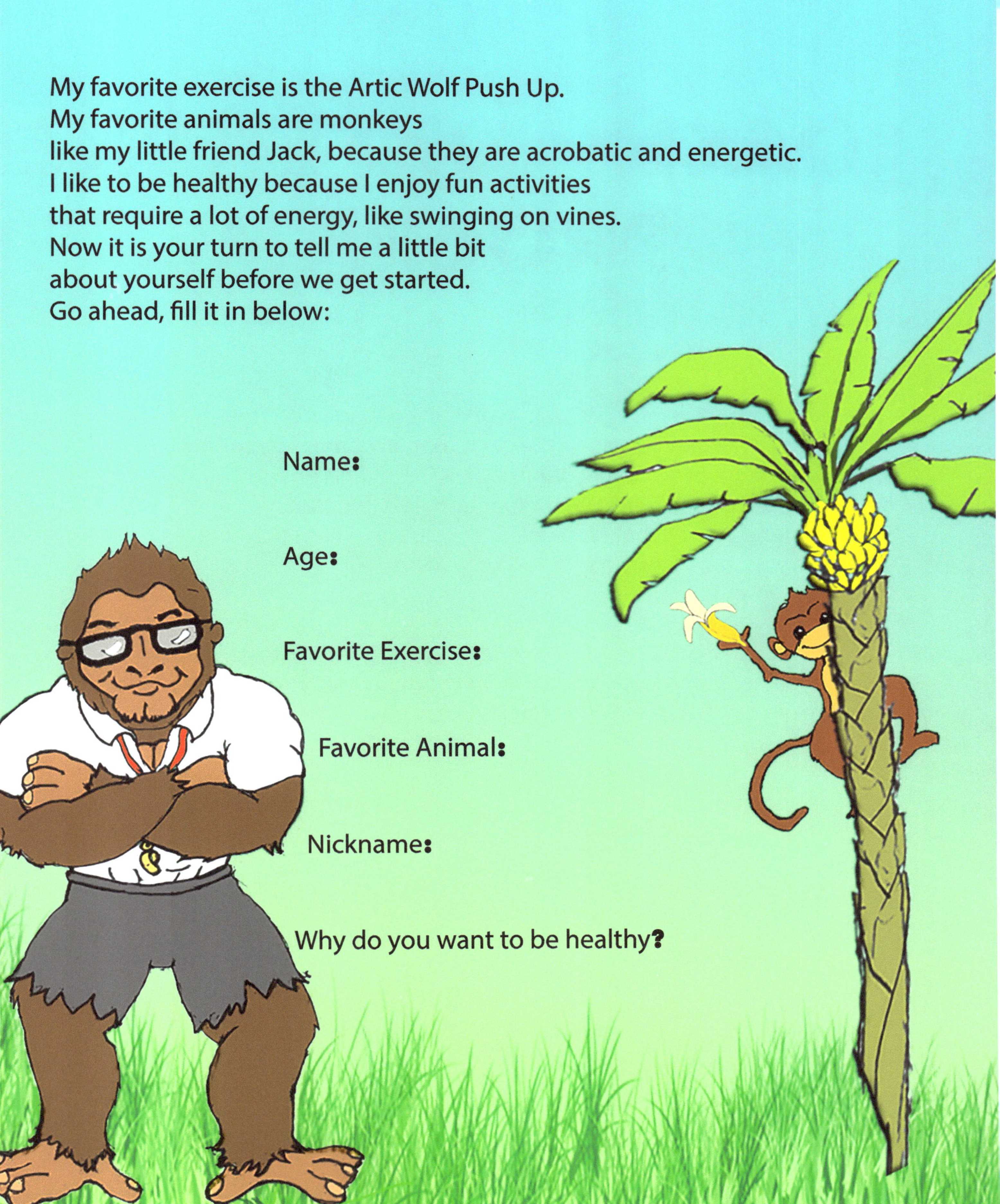

My favorite exercise is the Artic Wolf Push Up.
My favorite animals are monkeys
like my little friend Jack, because they are acrobatic and energetic.
I like to be healthy because I enjoy fun activities
that require a lot of energy, like swinging on vines.
Now it is your turn to tell me a little bit
about yourself before we get started.
Go ahead, fill it in below:

Name:

Age:

Favorite Exercise:

Favorite Animal:

Nickname:

Why do you want to be healthy?

COACH CONFIDENCE PROGRAM

Here is how my exercise program works. Every page describes an exercise. Do the exercise that you see on the page as many times as you can. When you are finished, mark your progress in the grid on the the right, like you see here. Every repetition gets counted. The next time you do that same exercise, you try to beat that score and write your new score in the next box over.

When you have practiced an exercise long enough, you can be confident you will master that exercise. You will feel better about your achievement and learn that nothing can stop you if you try your best.

At the end of every exercise, we celebrate by pounding our chests, like gorillas do, and saying:

"DO YOUR BEST AND POUND YOUR CHEST."

SCOREBOARD

Count how many times you perform an exercise and write your score on the scoreboard. Try to beat your score the next time you come back. You won't believe how much you can improve from your first score to your last. After you write your score, say our motto out loud:

"DO YOUR BEST AND POUND YOUR CHEST."

Get your family to pound their chest with you, IT'S FUN!

READY TO BEGIN?

Put your hand on mine,
count to three
and say,
"Work Hard."

1...2...3...

WORK HARD!

Stand up straight, reach down, and touch your toes.
If you don't want to stand,
sit down on the floor with straight legs
and reach for your toes.
This will improve your flexibility
and get you ready for what's to come.
The trick is to
not bend your knee and hold steady.

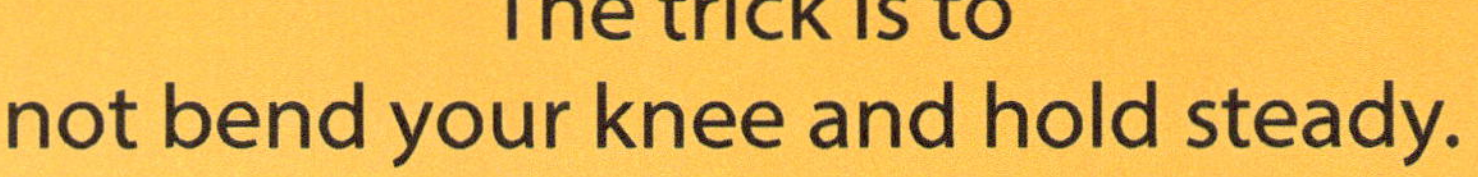

The Tiger Toe Touch is a stretch that improves our flexibility and takes pressure off our backs and knees. It prepares us for fun activities like chasing other gorillas, jumping, and squatting. It's your choice whether you stand or sit.

Don't forget to ROAR: "Do your best and pound your chest."

Our next exercise is the JUNGLE JUMPING JACK.
Start with your arms and legs straight down
like you are a pencil, then jump and
swing your arms and legs out wide
until you clap your hands above your head.
Swing your self back down, and that makes one.
Do as many as you can and don't stop.

Jungle Jumping Jacks are a fun and easy way to warm up the body and work on our cardiovascular system and coordination. Jungle Jumping Jacks can be done anytime and even though they get you warmed up, they won't wear you out.

Don't forget to SHOUT:
"Do your best and pound your chest."

CYCLONE ARM CIRCLES

Cyclones spin round and round, so do your arms.
Reach out wide, with straight arms, and make little circles.
Then swing them faster, and make the circles bigger
until your hands swing as high and as low as they can go.
Do this forwards and backwards, how long can you go?

We do arm circles to prepare our arms and shoulders for fun activities like swinging on vines, climbing up trees, throwing a ball, or doing push ups. They' are a great way to improve proprioception, balance and the cardiovascular system.

Don't forget to YELL:
"Do your best
and pound your chest."

ARCTIC WOLF PUSH UPS

Get down on your hands and toes, with your arms and body straight.
Bend at the elbows until you slowly lower your chest
to the ground. Keeping that body straight, push you body
back up to the starting position.

Artic Wolf Push Ups are my favortie exercise and make us super strong. We do push ups to improve our strength, which is our ability to move the world around us. Artic Wolf Push Ups are a great way to make yourself stronger and feel better!

Don't forget to EXCLAIM:
"Do your best and pound your chest!"

COBRA SIT UPS

Have a seat on the floor, bend your knees and lay back to the ground. Put your hands behind your head, squeeze your tummy and lift your chest up to your knees. Try not to let your feet leave the floor or straighten your knees out.

Sit Ups improve strength in the middle of our body.
This is important because the middle of our body, or "core,"
connects our lower body muscles and upper body muscles so
they can work together. Every strong gorilla has a strong core!

Don't forget to HISS:
"Do your best and pound your chest."

Lions are the king of the jungle, and squats are the king of exercises.
Bend your hips and knees at he same time. Keep
your back straight and tight through the whole movement.
Squat down until you are as low as
you can go with a straight back, then rise up the same way you
went down.

Lion squats are an excellent way to improve our strength.
Lower body strength will make you faster and less likely to fall.
Our legs take us everywhere we go, so it's very important
to make them as strong as we can. Squats improve strength
for your entire body!

Don't forget to ROAR:
"Do your best and pound your chest."

LIGHTNING PUNCHES

Have a partner hold a pillow or a cushion.
Keep hands up and cover your face. With one foot out,
punch first with your close hand and then your far hand.
Punch quick and hard, and cover your head
after each strike.

Don't forget to THUNDER:
"Do your best and pound your chest."

KANGAROO PUSH KICKS

Have a partner hold a pillow or cushion out in front of you. Standing up, raise one foot and kick the target with the bottom of your foot. Try to lift your knee up to your chest before you strike. Repeat this with both of your feet.

We kick a cushion, pillow, or heavy bag to
enhance balance, foot
coordination, and lower body conditioning.

Don't forget to SCREAM:
"Do your best and pound your chest."

GOAT MOUNTAIN CLIMBERS

Mountain Goat Climbers are like running in place. Put your hands on the ground right under your face with one foot straight back and the other on the ground under your hip. Without lifting your hands, quickly switch your feet back and forth. Keep going until you are too tired to stop.

Goat Mountain Climbers keep gorillas
and children quick and nimble.
They also work your cardiovascular system
and strengthen your core. They help you
stay in shape so you can roam the jungle
all day.

Don't forget to SAY:
"Do your best and pound your chest."

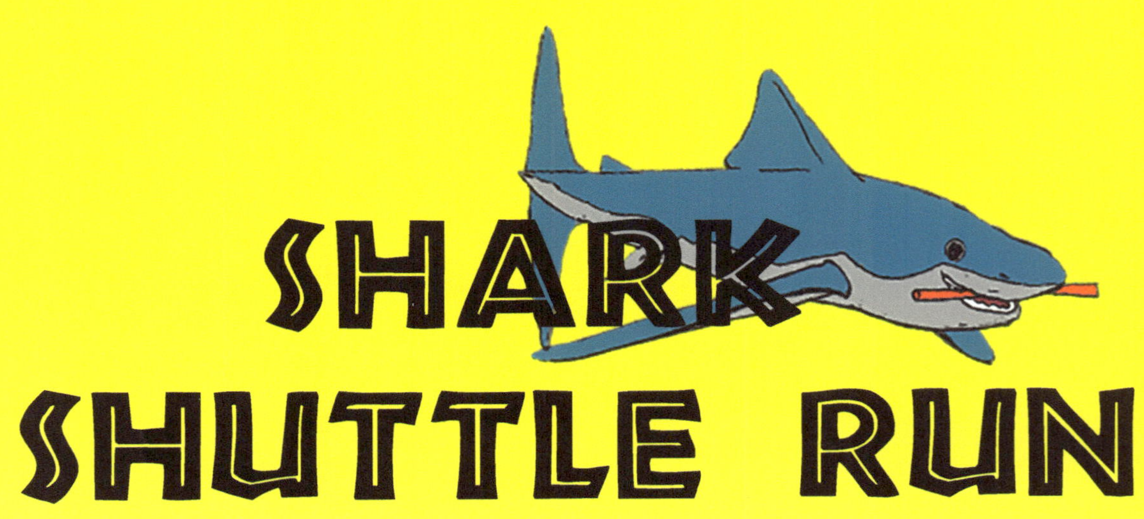

SHARK SHUTTLE RUN

Find a space to run fast.
Set an object down at one end,
then start from the other.
Run as fast as you can, pick up
the object and run back to the beginning.
Time it if you can, and always try to
beat your score.

Shuttle runs help you develop speed and agility.
It's a lot like Zig Zag Run, but you have the added challenge
of bending over, picking something up and
running straight for longer distances,
This will help you develop your speed and stamina.

Don't forget to HOLLER:
"Do your best and pound your chest."

ZIG ZAG ZEBRA RUN

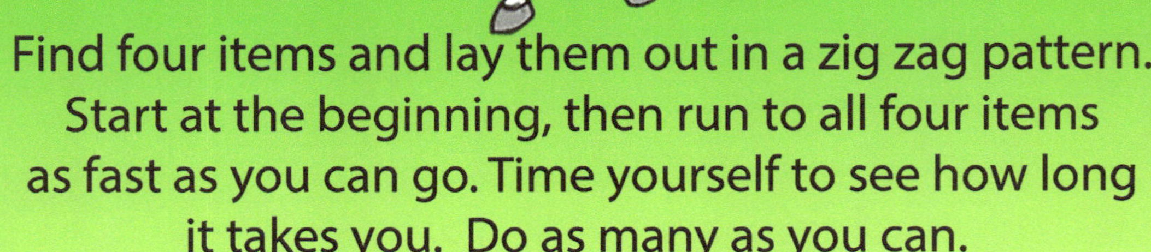

Find four items and lay them out in a zig zag pattern.
Start at the beginning, then run to all four items
as fast as you can go. Time yourself to see how long
it takes you. Do as many as you can.

Zig Zag runs train you to run fast in any direction without falling over or slowing down. This is an important skill for playtime or sports. When I play my favorite game, Gorilla Tag, I find myself running in zig zags all the time.

Don't forget to NEIGH:
"Do your best and pound your chest."

FROG JUMPS

Quickly hop back and forth on one leg,
then try it with the other leg.
You can do this side to side
and front to back.
One leg hops
are froggy like that.

A one-leg-hop is a fun way to learn more balance and coordination. When you go back to two legs, running and balancing will be easier. Plus, hopping on one leg makes you look like my favorite amphibian, the Central American tree frog!

Don't forget to HOLLER:
"Do your best and pound your chest."

HIPPO JUMP OVERS

Find something soft and safe to jump over.
Jump over it, land
and quickly jump back over.
You can start jumping side to side
over the object, then jump front
to back over the object. Do it quickly
and see how long you can go.

Jumping over something is a great way to work strength, balance and coordination in our legs. It also gets our heart beating faster, meaning it is a good aerobic activity.
Last but not least, jumping over something is fun.

Don't forget to SHOUT:
"Do your best and pound your chest."

PANDA
PITCH A BALL

Grab a ball and
put it in your dominant hand. Then
reach back and throw the ball, stepping
with your opposite foot. How close
can you get to the target? How far can
you throw? Make your throw a little
longer every day.

Everyone loves to throw a ball. Throwing a
ball is a fun and useful skill for most sports.
It's also a great way to make friends with other gorillas.
Throwing a ball improves our hand-eye coorrdination,
upper body strength and motor skils for our entire body.

Don't forget to GROWL:
"Do your best and pound your chest."

CROCODILE KICK

Grab any type of ball.
See the ball, chase the ball,
approach the ball, and kick the ball.
How far can you kick it?
Try to kick it with each of your feet.

Kicking the ball is a fun and useful skill for all children.
Kicking a ball requires you to balance on one foot while using all of
your muscles in your lower body. We kick a ball to work on balance,
motor skills, coordination and leg strength.

Don't forget to SCREAM:
"Do your best and pound your chest."

CONDOR CATCH

Find someone to throw you any type of ball and practice catching it. Have your hands out in front of your body, fingertips open, and watch the ball as it comes to you. Once the ball arrives, grab it and hold on as best as you can. How many can you do without dropping the ball?

Almost every sport, even soccer, has someone catching
a ball. The ball symbolizes opportunities, and we don't want
to miss our moment by dropping the ball. We catch a ball
to improve hand-eye coordination, depth perception, reaction time,
and quick-thinking skills.

Don't forget to SAY:
"Do your best and pound your chest."

FUEL

You have finished your exercises,
but you are not done yet.

This is Beanie, the health banana.
Do you see the three banana peels?
What do they say?

1. Exercise
2. Eat Healthy
3. Sleep Well

You just exercised, so make sure for the
rest of the day you eat healthy and
tonight you sleep well.
You will wake up in the morning ready
to do your best and pound your chest!

Next time you come back, try to beat all of your scores.
See you again tomorrow, same gorilla place and time.
Get on that gorilla routine.

CONGRATS!

You made it through today's exercises.

GORRRRRRRILLLLAAAAAAA
GRRRRREAAAAATTTT!!!!!!!!!!!!!!!!!!!!!

Pound your chest and draw
a star anywhere on this page.
Just don't cover my shades.